MIMESOPHOBIA

or

BEFORE AND AFTER

A reenactment by Carlos Murillo

BROADWAY PLAY PUBLISHING INC
New York
www.broadwayplaypublishing.com
info@broadwayplaypublishing.com

MIMESOPHOBIA
© Copyright 2015 by Carlos Murillo

.

First printing: November 2015
I S B N: 978-0-88145-640-0

Book design: Marie Donovan
Page make-up: Adobe Indesign
Typeface: Palatino
Printed and bound in the U S A

MIMESOPHOBIA (OR BEFORE AND AFTER) was
originally commissioned by South Coast Rep. Early
versions of it were developed at A S K Theater Projects,
South Coast Rep's Hispanic Playwrights Project, the
Chautauqua Institution Theater Conservatory, New
York Theater Workshop and Portland Center Stage's
JAW West Festival.

The play was first produced at the New York City
Summer Play Festival (Arielle Tepper, Executive
Producer). The production opened on 12 July 2005 at
the Samuel Beckett Theatre on Theatre Row with the
following cast and creative contributors:

SHAWN .... Florencia Lozano
JESSICA ....Lisa McCormick
WOMAN WHO SPEAKS... ....Kate Forbes
MAN WHO SPEAKS... .... Ezra Knight
HENRY ....Hamish Linklater
AARON..Lucas Caleb Rooney

Director.. Matt August,
Scenic design... Alexander Dodge
Lighting design ....Nicole Pearce
Sound design & original music .... Michael Creason
Costume design............................. Melissa Schlachtmeyer

The Chicago premiere of MIMESOPHOBIA (OR BEFORE AND AFTER) was produced by Theatre Seven, Brian Golden, Artistic Director. The production, directed by Margot Bordelon, opened on 4 March 2010 at Chicago Dramatists with the following cast and creative contributors:

SHAWN ....Cyd Blakewell
CASSY...Cassandra Sanders
WOMAN WHO SPEAKS... .... Jessica Thigpen
MAN WHO SPEAKS.......................................Brian Golden
HENRY .... Michael Salinas
AARON.. Brian Stojak

Director... Margot Bordelon
Scenic design...John Wilson
Lighting design .... Justin Wardell
Sound design.. Miles Polaski
Costume design.............Katie Cordts & Whitney McBride
Properties design.. Sarah Burnham
Composer...Chance Bone
Stage manager.......................................Taylor Fenderbosch

CHARACTERS

This play is to be performed by six actors—three women and three men. The roles are to be divided up as follows:

Woman #1: SHAWN

Woman #2: JESSICA
VOICE OF A DAUGHTER

Woman #3: WOMAN WHO SPEAKS IN THE THIRD PERSON OMNISCIENT *(aka.* KATE)
BETH

Man #1: MAN WHO SPEAKS BETWEEN THE SECOND AND THIRD PERSON OMNISCIENT *(aka* EZRA)
INTERVIEWER

Man #2: AARON MILLER

Man #3: HENRY BLUMENTHAL

A note: The actors playing JESSICA, WOMAN WHO SPEAKS IN THE 3RD PERSON OMNISCIENT *and the* MAN WHO SPEAKS BETWEEN THE 2ND & 3RD PERSON OMNISCIENT *should use their own, real first names in those roles.*

A double slash in the text indicates when the subsequent speech begins.

ACT ONE

Man Who Speaks Between The Second And Third
Person Omniscient: *(aka* Ezra*)*
Hi!
And welcome to
Mimesophobia
or
(before and after)
a reenactment by Carlos Murillo.
I'm the MAN WHO SPEAKS SOMEWHERE IN
BETWEEN THE SECOND AND THIRD PERSON
OMNISCIENT.
But
you can call me Ezra.

In a moment you'll hear the voice of the WOMAN
WHO SPEAKS IN THE SECOND PERSON
OMNISCIENT—a.k.a. Kate. She'll deliver the Prologue,
titled "PROLOGUE: before and after". Her lips will
practically caress your ear as she speaks to you in tones
that sooth. Calm. Reassure you that everything, yes,
everything's going to be okay.

Woman Who Speaks In The Second Person
Omniscient *(aka* Kate*)*:
You are sitting in one of the 2200 plush seats
in Grauman's Chinese Theatre in Hollywood.
Above you, to your sides, behind you
Exotic Asian motifs.
Dragons, gongs and other assorted Chinoiserie.

The theatre is dark,
except for the images projected onto the giant screen in
front of you.

You are watching the final scene of *before and after*
A new film by Aaron Miller and Henry Blumenthal,
Hollywood's latest wunderkinds.

This is a special night and you are a special guest:
Tonight is the film's world premiere screening.
You are not famous (you obtained your ticket through
a friend of a friend of a friend)
And even though you are just dark matter floating
through the universe
You feel contentto momentarily reflect the light
from the constellations of stars seated all around you.

Though attending film premieres might be unusual for
you,
Tonight most likely won't change your life.
Yes,
You might enjoy the film.
You might feel neither here nor there about it.
You might hate it, plain and simple.
But if you're lucky,
Later tonight,
When you curl up under the covers,
An image,
A phrase,
A moment from the film might find its way into your
dreams.
But no, tonight won't change your life.
Tomorrow you will most likely return to business as
usual.

So it doesn't cross your mind,
As you watch the final scene of *before and after* unfold
on screen,
That tonight marks an indelible line in time,

A line separating life before and life after
For at least two people in the audience.

Allow me to clarify what I mean by a line in time
separating life before and life after:
Imagine when you lost your virginity.
Imagine the day your mother died.
Imagine the moment you lost control of your car.
Imagine the day the Berlin Wall came down.
Imagine the moment you turned down the wrong
street, alone, late at night,
and your vulnerability attracted an unwanted stranger.
Imagine the moment he said, "I'm in love with you."
Imagine the moment she said, "I've met someone else."
Imagine the moment a mother loses her child.
Imagine the moment a mother gives birth.
I think you get the idea.
At this moment you might wonder, "Why?"
"Why go on with the play after reciting that litany of
befores and afters—
Each incantation has thoroughly exercised my
imagination,
A few triggered memories I'd rather forget.
Some provoked a sense of dread I'd rather not feel
right now."
While that may be true,
I want to point out that not every line in time
separating life before and life after
is so indelible.
Unlike the loss of virginity, death of a parent, great
historical moment, birth of
a child,
There exists an invisible before and after:
Where the separating line does not etch the
consciousness,
But disappears into the vast sea of mundane and
unremarkable memory.

Tonight—
As you sit in Grauman's Chinese Theatre in
Hollywood,
Watching the final scene of *before and after* unfold—
Marks such a line.
For you the line might be invisible.
But for the two young men that made the film,
Aaron Miller and Henry Blumenthal,
The line is indelible.
The film, you see, will be a huge success.
Their lives before as fledgling auteurs have come to an
end.
Their lives after are just beginning.
Watch: The final scene of the film unfolds on screen.
Henry and Aaron will tell you what you see.

HENRY: Exterior. OSCAR and MARISOL's Prairie Style
house in Hyde Park, Chicago. January. Night.

The windows of the house are dark. We track towards
the house, towards one of the windows, closer and
closer until we pass through it.

AARON: REVERSE ANGLE

Interior. The dining room, mostly in shadow, except for
shapeless pools of light formed by streetlamps outside
and headlights of passing traffic. The camera slowly
tracks backwards revealing: the dining room table.

HENRY: Spread out on the table, a lavish banquet.
Fine china, neatly arranged antique silverware.
Untouched. Row after row of crystal champagne flutes.
Unsipped from. Hors d'oerves. Unsampled. A roast, a
glazed ham, a garnished turkey worthy of a gourmet
magazine centerfold, a basket with exotic fruit.
Uneaten. An elaborate sculptured tower of confections.
Undisturbed.

AARON: And the centerpiece: a roasted suckling pig
with a blood red apple impaled in its mouth.

HENRY: Uncarved

AARON: There's a haunted stillness in the room.

HENRY: As if the feast has given up waiting for guests to indulge in it.

AARON: We track through other rooms, also dark. From a far corner of the house we see the dim illumination of a reading lamp and bluish light from a television.

HENRY: We move towards it, closer and closer, until we arrive at it's source: the den.

AARON: OSCAR sits in a leather reading chair, a book on his lap, an unlit Cohiba cigar wedged between his middle and fore finger. He stares, dazed, into the space between his eyes and the carpet. Gone is his usual youthful vigor, ironic demeanor and the proud carriage of a hugely successful academic. His age is apparent, as if for the first time. It's not just that his face is grave, it's that it's become a gravestone.

HENRY: OSCAR's wife MARISOL lies on her stomach on the couch, disheveled. She's finished by herself the empty bottle of Merlot that sits on the side table. Her arm dangles limply off the edge, fingers grazing the stem of the wine glass, which lies on its side, empty, except for a few drops of the Merlot, which savagely contrast the white of the carpet.

AARON: Except for MARISOL's soft crying, the room is silent. Television is on, volume muted, tuned to the local P B S station, moments before the evening's broadcast of Charlie Rose. We see the opening credits, helicopter shot over the nighttime New York City skyline.
CUT TO:

HENRY: Long shot of the room. MARISOL and OSCAR, backs to us, and the television set all in frame. They don't notice the show has started. CHARLIE ROSE,

begins the introduction of his guest, mouthing many words, holding up a copy of the guest's new book. He nods to the guest across the table from him, who we only see from behind.
CUT TO:

AARON: Closeup of MARISOL, who lifts her head slightly, cheeks stained with tears, to catch a glimpse of the image on screen. Her face transforms from bloated mourning to cold hard stone. Eyes deadening with unwanted recognition. She turns to OSCAR.
CUT TO:

HENRY: Medium shot: OSCAR, feeling the wave of hatred coming from MARISOL, looks up at her. He's never seen her eyes so steely, unforgiving. He turns to the television and sees on screen SHAWN. She's radiant. Alluring. Looking smart as hell, reveling in Charlie Rose's attentions.
CUT TO:

AARON: Close up of OSCAR's face. If his face was a gravestone before, it's now a mausoleum. We move slowly down to a close up of the hand that holds the cigar.
CUT TO:

HENRY: Long shot of the room. MARISOL struggles to her feet, stumbles tipsy to the T V. She reaches to turn it off, but thinks better of it, maximizing the cruelty of the moment. She stumbles to the telephone table next to OSCAR's chair. She jabs the play button on the answering machine. She stumbles out of the room. We hear

AARON: OSCAR & MARISOL'S
MURDERED
DAUGHTER'S
VOICE on the machine.

A message she left just hours
before she was brutally murdered by her husband.

VOICE OF DAUGHTER ON MACHINE: Hey Dad, hey
mom, it's me.
Wanted to let you know we are flying in for the
party—
Hope it isn't too last minute but we figured...
Our flight leaves tomorrow at three from Boston so we
should be in...
sometime around five I guess?
Don't bother picking us up at the airport—we'll just
rent a car.

AARON: CUT TO:
Closeup of the unlit cigar in OSCAR's fingers.

VOICE OF DAUGHTER ON MACHINE: God, I can't wait to
see you both.
We have some amazing news for you...
Don't try calling back to ask... I want to keep you in
suspense.

AARON: OSCAR's middle and forefinger go limp. The
cigar slips from them and drops in slow motion onto
the carpet, like the rotor of a doomed helicopter.
CUT TO:

HENRY: Long shot of the room. OSCAR with his back
to us, alone, cigar on the carpet, television on, muted.
On screen, SHAWN glows. We hear a beep indicating
the end of the phone message. Silence. We slowly
pull out of the den, track backwards through the dark
rooms of the house, past the untouched feast and out
the window, into the dark, freezing Chicago night.
Everything goes black.

AARON: The End.

WOMAN WHO SPEAKS IN THE SECOND PERSON
OMNISCIENT: *(aka* KATE) For a moment—like the rest of

the audience
in Grauman's Chinese Theatre in Hollywood,
you sit in silence.
As the tense, dissonant motifs of the film score break
the silence,
And the closing credits start to roll,
You join in the enthusiastic burst of applause.

1

WOMAN WHO SPEAKS IN THE SECOND PERSON
OMNISCIENT: *(aka* KATE*)* Now that the Prologue's done
let's start scene one shall we?

Listen: we hear the voice of the MAN WHO SPEAKS
SOMEWHERE IN BETWEEN THE SECOND AND
THIRD PERSON OMNISCIENT—a.k.a. Ezra. Note his
measured, self-assured, yet humble tone, reassuring
you that everything, yes, everything's going to be okay.

MAN WHO SPEAKS SOMEWHERE IN BETWEEN THE
SECOND AND THIRD PERSON OMNISCIENT: *(aka* EZRA*)*
Thanks, Kate.
Why don't we step over here and meet Shawn.

That's her lying on the bed.

You'll notice it's one of eleven twin beds sandwiched
into a dormitory room of an artist's colony in Southern
California. You'll notice the dorm's ramshackle
charm—
(the retreat house originally catered to Christian youth
groups—Methodists to be precise)
Writers, artists, composers, academics from all over the
world come to the colony to
retreat
from the pressures of day to day existence –
It's a place for
contemplation.

Regeneration.
Creation.
And because the colony welcomes folks of various
disciplines:
cross-pollination.
All of which enables the colonists to "think outside the
box"....

Shawn is here attempting to finish a *book*
She'd been writing for three and a half years.
She came to the colony explicitly to write the seventh
chapter
The chapter she needed to complete in order to finish
the book.

SHAWN: The middle chapter
The keystone.
The magic shard of kryptonite.
The cat burglar's pick that once turned will drop the
tumblers in place
Opening a door...

MAN WHO SPEAKS SOMEWHERE IN BETWEEN THE
SECOND AND THIRD PERSON OMNISCIENT: *(aka* EZRA*)*
If you look closely at the woman in the bed
you might see a resemblance to the Shawn from the
film—
the film you watched in the prologue?
remember the Charlie Rose segment?
Though no one would hold it against you if you *didn't*
recognize her.
Because the Shawn you see here is a very different
Shawn
From the one in the film:
Whereas in the film's Charlie Rose sequence she
radiated
movie star glamour, a naughty wit, a towering
intelligence,
the picture you see here is more a

badly lit candid, an
unflattering Polaroid
A
"Before"
picture of her, if you will.

Shawn might appear to you like she's dead
Or near death
The way she stares up at the ceiling.
Chestnut hair wild and spread out over the pillow.
Pale.
Faraway look in her eyes.
Arms in a tangle around her head.
And the little black tape recorder she holds in her left
hand.
Oh wait: she's raising the tape recorder to her mouth.

SHAWN: Notes on Chapter Seven:
"Bullet Through a Disguise
(colon)
(subtitle)
Chung Ling Soo and the Bullet Catch Effect"

Though many variations of the Bullet Catch Effect have
been performed over the years, the basic idea is the
same:
a loaded rifle is fired directly at the illusionist by an
assistant.
The illusionist, in the split second after the gun shot,
catches the bullet either in his teeth or on a plate *(why a
plate, I wonder?)*.

According to Ben Robinson, magician and author of
Twelve Have Died (Ray Goulet's Magic Art Book Co.
1986—out of print), at least twelve recorded deaths
have been attributed to this Effect.

The first reference to the Bullet Catch, according to
Robinson, appears in the 1597 volume, *Theatre of God's*

Judgments by Reverend Thomas Beard. *(Subsequent editions 1612, 1631, 1648.)*

Note to self: Beard's account must be taken with the proverbial grain of salt. In spite of Beard's zealous Puritanism, he was not above baroque narrative embroidery, wild historical revisionism, gruesome and lurid embellishment, half-truths and outright lies, in his chronicle of history's spectacular examples of divine vengeance.

Anyway: The reference concerns Coulen, a French illusionist who attempted the Effect in 1550. His attempt was successful. However, one spectator, horrified by the illusionist's Luciferian defiance of God's will to give and take life, tore the gun from Coulen's assistant, and proceeded to beat Coulen to death with it.

MAN WHO SPEAKS SOMEWHERE IN BETWEEN THE SECOND AND THIRD PERSON OMNISCIENT: *(aka* EZRA*)*
Wait: she's clicked off the recorder.

SHAWN: Yeah…that's all well and good but…
That's just the exposition.

MAN WHO SPEAKS SOMEWHERE IN BETWEEN THE SECOND AND THIRD PERSON OMNISCIENT: *(aka* EZRA*)*
Let me clarify: the Shawn you see here, of course is not the *real* Shawn
No more than the Shawn you saw in the movie was the *real* Shawn
The *real* Shawn is…
Well
since her mysterious disappearance…
no one really knows for sure where she is…

Ah! Meet Shawn's mother
Beth.

Now: the real Beth couldn't be with us today so…

Kate?

WOMAN WHO SPEAKS IN THE SECOND PERSON
OMNISCIENT: *(aka* KATE*)* Yes Ezra.

MAN WHO SPEAKS SOMEWHERE IN BETWEEN THE
SECOND AND THIRD PERSON OMNISCIENT: *(aka* EZRA*)*
Would you do the honors?

WOMAN WHO SPEAKS IN THE SECOND PERSON
OMNISCIENT: *(aka* KATE*)* Of course.

BETH: That's Shawn
My daughter
Lying on the bed.

MAN WHO SPEAKS SOMEWHERE IN BETWEEN THE
SECOND AND THIRD PERSON OMNISCIENT: *(aka* EZRA*)*
I realize how
difficult this must be for you.

BETH: It is. It really, really is.

MAN WHO SPEAKS SOMEWHERE IN BETWEEN THE
SECOND AND THIRD PERSON OMNISCIENT: *(aka* EZRA*)*
We appreciate you traveling so far to be with us.

BETH: Thank you for having me I—
My God. She looks just like Shawn how did you—
Why is she pale?
Why does she look dead?

MAN WHO SPEAKS SOMEWHERE IN BETWEEN THE
SECOND AND THIRD PERSON OMNISCIENT: *(aka* EZRA*)*
Care to tell us a little bit about your daughter?

BETH: Shawn and I
We
Don't talk much maybe
Once twice in
Ohhh
Probably the uhhh
Last five years?

But Shawn's very busy so I understand her
Um
Not staying in touch
and as her mother I will say that uhhh
despite the estrangement
maybe estrangement is too strong a word but
despite our not talking or seeing one another too often
I
Am
Proud.
Of her.

MAN WHO SPEAKS SOMEWHERE IN BETWEEN THE
SECOND AND THIRD PERSON OMNISCIENT: (aka EZRA)
Anyway:
In the months prior to arriving at the colony
Shawn was suffering a severe case of writer's block
She came to the colony explicitly to write the seventh
chapter
of a book she'd been working on for three and a half
years.
The chapter she needed to complete in order to finish
the book.

SHAWN: The middle chapter
The keystone.
The magic shard of kryptonite.
The cat burglar's pick that once turned will drop the
tumblers in place
Opening a door...

MAN WHO SPEAKS SOMEWHERE IN BETWEEN THE
SECOND AND THIRD PERSON OMNISCIENT: (aka EZRA)
Completing the seventh chapter however
Was the source of terror for Shawn.
She procrastinated.
Made excuses.
Engaged in unnecessary, redundant research.

She'd already written her dissertation on the same
subject.
See: even though this was Shawn's first book,
She was battling a severe case of Mimesophobia
Which means
For those of you who don't know
"The morbid fear of slavish imitation"

So in the midst of her procrastination, redundant
research,
Shawn woke up one morning –
Hung over from drinking heavily,
And bit the bullet, as it were,
By accepting a residency at the artist's colony.

BETH: She called me out of the blue one day to tell me
she was going away
I said "But Sandy, you're always away. Why the call?"

She gets mad
Really.
Mad.
when I call her that. Sandy.
But what can I do?
That's her real name.
She made up Shawn her sophomore year in high
school.
I remember the day it happened.
She came home from school,
Walked into the kitchen
Put her briefcase down
(she wanted a leather briefcase to differentiate herself from all
the kids with backpacks)
I said "Hi Sandy, how was your—"

SHAWN: Mother…
You are no longer to address me as Sandy.
Henceforth you will address me by my name. Shawn.
Ess-aitch-ay-double u-en. Shawn.

BETH: That's what she said
"Address me by my name."
She even spelled it for me.
I didn't give her that name.
I would never have given her that name.
I generally dislike women with boy's names.
And I have to say I was pretty insulted and
hurt.
What was wrong with the name I gave her?
I mean... it was my first gift to her, you know?
To have her throw it back in my face like that just...

But she was always a peculiar child.
From that day forward our
relationship was never quite the same.

MAN WHO SPEAKS SOMEWHERE IN BETWEEN THE
SECOND AND THIRD PERSON OMNISCIENT: *(aka* EZRA*)*
Okay....

BETH: Anyhow: She called me out of the blue and said
she was going away

SHAWN: Mother I'm going away.

BETH: "But sweetie, I don't know where you are now,
why are you calling me to tell me you're going away?"
And she said:

SHAWN: Fine. You don't want to talk to me. I'll hang
up. That's fine.

BETH: And I said, "No no no no sweetie. I'm so happy
to hear your voice.
But seeing as you never call I just...
Is something wrong?"

SHAWN: No
nothing's wrong.
Why are you always so negative?!?!?
I'm just telling you that I'm going away.

BETH: That's nice darling.

SHAWN: I'm going away to finish my book.

BETH: A book! I didn't know you were writing a book, that's wonderful dear.

SHAWN: It's got a title.

BETH: That's wonderful.

SHAWN: Don't you want to know what the title is?

BETH: Of course dear. Tell me the title.

SHAWN: One Night Only

BETH: That's a wonderful title what's the book //
about

SHAWN: I'm. Not. Finished.

(Long pause)

SHAWN: That's only part of the title. The title is
followed by a colon
followed by a subtitle.
Do you want to know what the title after the colon is?

BETH: Of course dear.

SHAWN: Or are you just going to pretend you're
listening.

BETH: I'm listening sweetie. I assure you. Mama's all
ears.

SHAWN: Okay.
Here goes.
Are you sure you're listening?

(Long silence.)

SHAWN: One Night Only
(colon)
(subtitle)
Actual Death
and the Future
of American

Entertainment.

(Silence)

BETH: That's

im

pressive

dear.

(Long pause)

SHAWN: I'm calling you
Because I wanted to tell you
That I'm almost done.

BETH: That's...

SHAWN: I have one more chapter to go.

BETH: Oh, that's that's...

SHAWN: Chapter seven.
The keystone.
The magic shard of kryptonite.
The cat burglar's pick that once turned will drop the
tumblers in place
Opening a door....

BETH: Does it have a title?

SHAWN: Yes,
Beth
In fact it also has a title.

BETH: Tell me.
What
is it?

SHAWN: Well,
Beth

BETH: Sweetie—

SHAWN: The title of the chapter is:
Bullet Through a Disguise

BETH: I see.

SHAWN: *I'm not finished*
Beth.

BETH: Does it also have a colon and a subtitle?

SHAWN: Yes,
Beth
In fact it does and if you paid attention to anything
other than your own neuroses
I might tell you.

BETH: I'm all ears.

SHAWN: Yeah, well fuck you *Beth* if you think / / I'm
gonna tell you.

BETH: SANDY STOP CALLING ME BETH I AM YOUR
MOTHER I NEVER ALLOWED YOU TO CALL ME
BY MY FIRST NAME I NEVER ALLOWED ANY OF
MY CHILDREN TO CALL ME BY MY FIRST NAME!!!!

SHAWN: *(laughing)*
You are so pathetic
Mom.

BETH: She hung up…
That's the last I heard of her until….

MAN WHO SPEAKS SOMEWHERE IN BETWEEN THE
SECOND AND THIRD PERSON OMNISCIENT: *(aka* EZRA*)*
Until…?

BETH: I mean I really didn't think about it at the time
but
Her calling me?
Out of the blue like that I…?
Was she…
Maybe…?
Maybe she was
trying to tell me something…?

who knew she would just....
Vanish into thin air like that.

MAN WHO SPEAKS SOMEWHERE IN BETWEEN THE
SECOND AND THIRD PERSON OMNISCIENT: *(aka EZRA)*
The gentlemen you see here—Henry and Aaron they
um...

Hi guys.

AARON & HENRY: Hey.

MAN WHO SPEAKS SOMEWHERE IN BETWEEN THE
SECOND AND THIRD PERSON OMNISCIENT: *(aka EZRA)*
In one of nature's strange and fortuitous coincidences
Henry and Aaron's stay at the colony coincided with
Shawn's,
They were at work on a screenplay.
You might have seen the resulting film? *before and after?*
Yes, the film praised by *The New York Times* for its
"unflinching portrait of a seemingly successful modern
marriage torn asunder by the rot of infidelity, secrets
and lies."

HENRY: Based on a true-life murder/suicide.

AARON: Though I think it's important to point out we
fictionalized
certain parts to enhance the film's
drama,
suspense.

HENRY: They don't need to know that Aaron. Why do
they // need to

MAN WHO SPEAKS SOMEWHERE IN BETWEEN THE
SECOND AND THIRD PERSON OMNISCIENT: *(aka EZRA)*
Let me clarify that like the Shawn you see lying on the
bed,
These gentlemen are not the real Aaron Miller and
Henry Blumenthal—
The real Aaron and Henry are....

HENRY: We're fucking famous now.

MAN WHO SPEAKS SOMEWHERE IN BETWEEN THE
SECOND AND THIRD PERSON OMNISCIENT: *(aka* EZRA*)*
That's right.

AARON: Communal meals were supposed to be a
highlight of the colonists' time at the retreat,
Opportunity to
Talk shop, compare notes,
"cross-pollinate"
That sort of thing.
Least that's what the founders of the place intended.

HENRY: They were a drag and the food sucked.

AARON: Anyway, Henry and I got to know Shawn
pretty well at these meals

HENRY: I'd say you got to know her pretty well in
circumstances other than meals

AARON: Shut up. Anyway—
For some reason
Shawn always chose to sit at our table.

HENRY: Her and that whacked out composer from
Albania

AARON: Which was weird cause she never talked to us,
she would just sit there eating a stack of tortillas she'd
spread with peanut butter. That's all she ate, breakfast
lunch and dinner, peanut butter tortillas. After about a
week I started getting tense about the whole situation,
sitting there with my partner, those two freaks not
saying a word—Shawn eating tortillas, the Albanian
composer guy humming all dissonant while he chewed
his food real loud.
Finally at breakfast one day I said:
"So I...
Read in the welcome packet that uhh...
You're writing a book."

She looked, stared at me for what seemed like forever,
with those weird vacant eyes of hers. And she said.

SHAWN: Yeah.

AARON: That was it. Back to the same old silence until
like five minutes later
After she'd downed her third peanut butter tortilla she
looked up
Stared blankly at me again and started talking all

Catatonic.

SHAWN: The book's called
One Night Only
(colon)
(subtitle)
Actual Death
and the Future of American Entertainment.

HENRY: Awesome title.

SHAWN: It's a
critical examination of the history of entertainment in
America
Specifically forms of entertainment designed to titillate
audiences
With the promise of possible, actual, death.

AARON: Whoa.

SHAWN: Not the audience's possible death
but rather the possible death of the entertainers
themselves
Though in certain cases the lives of spectators share
this possible destiny

HENRY: So true

SHAWN: I'd written my dissertation on pretty much the
same subject.
Only
I didn't want that version published.

Despite the
protestations
Despite the
"counsel"
of my

"Mentor"

I

wanted to reach a more
General
Audience.
More
"think piece"
Less
academic tract.
Geared to
readers of *The New Yorker*.
Harper's.
Devotees of
Charlie Rose.
That sort of thing.
I've been working on it for three and a half years.
I'm
trying to
finish
chapter seven.

AARON: I see.

SHAWN: Yes.
Chapter seven:
"Bullet Through a Disguise
(colon)
(subtitle)
"Chung Ling Soo and the Bullet Catch Effect"

HENRY: Chung Ling Who?

SHAWN: Chung Ling *Soo*, Marvelous Chinese Conjurer.
(Not to be confused with Ching Ling Foo)

AARON: Yeah, I think I might have heard of him isn't
he the guy

SHAWN: Yes. Thing is though:

AARON: She leaned forward and whispered:

SHAWN: He wasn't really Chinese

AARON: Then she leaned back, started talking normal
again—if you can call it normal.

SHAWN: His real name was Ellsworth Robinson.
He was a Scotsman from Brooklyn.

AARON: Then she leaned forward, whispered again:

SHAWN: *He only pretended he was Chinese.*

AARON: Then back to "normal":

SHAWN: It's the last chapter I need to write.
The keystone.
The magic shard of kryptonite.
The cat burglar's pick that once turned will drop the
tumblers in place
Opening a door…

AARON: After that the verbal floodgates opened—
Still catatonic-like, but
She just wouldn't shut up about it
She talked in this unnerving monotone
Like she was afraid the words she was saying might
kill her.
She told us there were chapters on auto racing

HENRY: Harry Houdini

AARON: The phenomenon of so-called reality television

HENRY: The nightly news

AARON: Televised police chases on California freeways

HENRY: Evel Kneivel

AARON: Vigils staged for death row inmates facing execution

HENRY: Extreme sports

AARON: The television show *When Animals Attack*

HENRY: *World's Deadliest Police Chases*

AARON: And that these chapters are craftily arranged
to argue a controversial thesis
Namely, that for spectators
There exists a natural inclination to slow down on highways
to gawk at a wreck on the opposite lane.

HENRY: Twisted metal, flashing police cruiser lights, rush of emer//gency vehicles

AARON: The long and the short of her thesis was:
Since rubbernecking is a natural inclination for viewers
It is the moral duty of T V producers to satisfy it to the most extreme ends.

SHAWN: Executions must be televised.
They should be like State of the Union addresses.
Preempting regular programming,
Shown from start to finish
It's only logical.

AARON: I was pretty blown away by the craziness of what she was saying? so
real gentle I asked whether she believed this in her heart of hearts,
Or if she was just playing devil's advocate to provoke a discussion on
the death penalty, T V violence, etc....

There was this silence, after which she looked at me in this weirdly vulnerable way and said:

SHAWN: Well. You'll just have to read carefully in between the lines, now, won't you?

If you'll excuse me: I have a date with a fake Chinaman.

AARON: She rolled up her remaining tortillas and disappeared upstairs.

2

WOMAN WHO SPEAKS IN THE SECOND PERSON OMNISCIENT: *(aka* KATE*)* Now seems like an appropriate time to segue into scene two.

MAN WHO SPEAKS SOMEWHERE IN BETWEEN THE SECOND AND THIRD PERSON OMNISCIENT: *(aka* EZRA*)*
A scene in which Jessica,
Youngest daughter of Oscar and Marisol,
reconstructs
the contents of her murdered sister's diary.
That's Jessica over there.
And yes ladies and gentlemen: *un*like
the Oscar and Marisol you saw portrayed in the film
the Jessica you see is the
Real
Jessica.
Jessica is the youngest of Oscar and Marisol's *two*
daughters,
made an only child by her older sister's murderer.

WOMAN WHO SPEAKS IN THE SECOND PERSON OMNISCIENT: *(aka* KATE*)* Ezra…

MAN WHO SPEAKS SOMEWHERE IN BETWEEN THE SECOND AND THIRD PERSON OMNISCIENT: *(aka* EZRA*)*
While not quite the black sheep of her family,
She also is not quite her father's daughter.

WOMAN WHO SPEAKS IN THE SECOND PERSON
OMNISCIENT: *(aka* KATE*)* Ezra…

MAN WHO SPEAKS SOMEWHERE IN BETWEEN THE
SECOND AND THIRD PERSON OMNISCIENT: *(aka* EZRA*)*
At the time of her sister's murder,
Jessica was about to enter her sixth year
Of a three-year Master's Degree Program in Art
Restoration
at the University of New Mexico, Albuquerque.

WOMAN WHO SPEAKS IN THE SECOND PERSON
OMNISCIENT: *(aka* KATE*)* Ezra…

MAN WHO SPEAKS SOMEWHERE IN BETWEEN THE
SECOND AND THIRD PERSON OMNISCIENT: *(aka* EZRA*)*
Needless to say,
her experience in the painstaking process of
reconstructing endangered works of art
aided Jessica in the reconstruction of her sister's
diary—
though of course a diary is almost never a work of art.

WOMAN WHO SPEAKS IN THE SECOND PERSON
OMNISCIENT: *(aka* KATE*)* Ezra.

MAN WHO SPEAKS SOMEWHERE IN BETWEEN THE
SECOND AND THIRD PERSON OMNISCIENT: *(aka* EZRA*)*
Yes Kate.

WOMAN WHO SPEAKS IN THE SECOND PERSON
OMNISCIENT: *(aka* KATE*)* Maybe we should
Step back a little.
Let her tell her story.

MAN WHO SPEAKS SOMEWHERE IN BETWEEN THE
SECOND AND THIRD PERSON OMNISCIENT: *(aka* EZRA*)*
Of course.

JESSICA: My voice sounds a lot—
sound*ed*
a lot like my sister's. People confused us all the time.

Even Mom and Dad would confuse us when we called
them in Chicago.

Dad still does that sometimes.
When I call he'll call me by her name and
then there's
just this awful silence.

When the authorities informed me that my sister had
kept a diary?
It kind of knocked the wind out of me I mean who
would have known....

See: my sister she had a
Certainty?
About her?
She approached everything in life with this
Ferocious certainty—from when we were kids, through
school, college grad school marrying when she did *who*
she did—at least who he seemed to be...
It's like the entire supply of the certainty gene went
straight from my dad to her
Bypassing me completely.
I know to a certain extent she was imitating dad who,
let's face it
doesn't have an ounce of self doubt in his body...
But...
She imitated him well.
Probably too well.

Given all that I was surprised she kept a diary—her—
of all people...
Keeping a diary to me always implied a kind of
Introspection
I didn't think my sister had
I always thought in our family? I had a monopoly of
that particular gene...

To think he made her watch him tear out the pages and
throw them into the fire... he incinerated my sister's

soul...the fragile truth that lay hidden inside her—
unseen by me, unseen by anyone in our family...

He incinerated that.

The forensic team found
charred fragments of
of her diary in the ashes of the fireplace—
And um...
Two pages—
barely legible for being wrinkled and
blood soaked from
from her clutching them in her hands,
as if she was trying to save them before...

Aside from those fragments there's

nothing left of her....

So I've tried to *reconstruct*
I've tried to
Fill in the gaping holes
I've had to
imagine
the contents
of that diary.

3

MAN WHO SPEAKS SOMEWHERE IN BETWEEN THE
SECOND AND THIRD PERSON OMNISCIENT: *(aka* EZRA*)*
Shhhh.... Listen:
The inmates at the colony are getting restless. Look:
Shawn talks into her tape recorder.

SHAWN: Woke up this morning six fifteen.
Two hours forty-seven minutes of sleep.
Fucked up dreams starring who else but:
Chung Ling Soo.
Woke up feeling

Claustrophobic.
Walls of the room seem
More closed in than yesterday.
Doorway eerie, like something shadowy
Malevolent
Lurking just behind it.

I'm in need of a change of scenery.
Otherwise
I think I might just

You know....

Maybe at breakfast I'll ask one of the other inmates
if I could borrow their car.

MAN WHO SPEAKS SOMEWHERE IN BETWEEN THE
SECOND AND THIRD PERSON OMNISCIENT: *(aka* EZRA*)*
Breakfast. SHAWN. AARON. And HENRY. And yes,
the WHACKED OUT ALBANIAN COMPOSER. Listen
to him hum all dissonant while chewing his food.
Watch SHAWN. She spreads thick gobs of peanut
butter onto a tortilla.

AARON: So: how was your date with the fake
Chinaman?

SHAWN: What
Did you
Say?

AARON: Chung Ling....

It was a
joke

SHAWN: I don't know about you gentlemen but
I'm in need a change of scenery.
Otherwise
I think I might just…

Never mind.

AARON: Yeah, I know what you mean.

SHAWN: Do you?

AARON: I'm going a little stir crazy myself.

SHAWN: You are?

(Beat)

I was thinking of
Maybe
Driving.
Into Los Angeles.
I've never been to Los Angeles before.

(Pause)

Problem being I
don't have a car.

(Pause)

AARON: I have a car

SHAWN: Oh.
I was thinking
Maybe
If you were feeling
You know
Stir crazy
Maybe you'd

HENRY: Dude, what are you talking about?

AARON: What?

HENRY: You're not thinking of leaving.

AARON: C'mon Henry we've been locked up in that
room for days.

HENRY: We're making progress.

AARON: Yeah, but…

HENRY: Dude, no "yeah, buts".
Dude, this is no time to go stir crazy.
Dude, we're almost on a roll.

AARON: I know. I know. But still…

HENRY: Dude, you fuckin drop the ball on this one….

AARON: I'm not dropping the ball…

SHAWN: Sorry I brought it up.
Look…
If you're not using it?
I wondered?
If maybe…
Maybe you'll loan me your car?

MAN WHO SPEAKS SOMEWHERE IN BETWEEN THE
SECOND AND THIRD PERSON OMNISCIENT: *(aka* EZRA*)*
Watch: male fantasy—Aaron's inner movie as he
imagines Shawn tearing up the California freeways:

AARON: Helicopter shot of a 1972 Mercedes, snaking
through traffic on the 405
Moving at a frightening rate of speed. CUT TO
Shot from the rear seat—Back of Shawn's head, relaxed
hand on the wheel,
gleam in her eye visible as a reflection in the rear view
mirror.
Speedometer needle fixed at 120 miles an hour.

Yowwwww. Better call Nina quick.

MAN WHO SPEAKS SOMEWHERE IN BETWEEN THE
SECOND AND THIRD PERSON OMNISCIENT: *(aka* EZRA*)*
Listen: Beth provides the voiceover:

BETH: I can just imagine my daughter on the freeway,
driving into Los Angeles with that
Apocalyptic smile on her face.

She wrote me a postcard.
Picture of that movie theatre—the one all done up like
a fake Chinese palace?
She wrote, in the tiniest handwriting:

BETH & SHAWN: Dear Mom. This city makes me feel alive in ways few cities do. On a day to day basis

SHAWN: the city dweller imagines her surroundings as permanent—something that has been for a long time and will be for a long time, long after the city dweller's relocation to the necropolis. This sense of permanence is one among the billion white lies the city dweller must tell herself in order to go on with "business as usual".
In order to function as a normal, productive human being.

But in this city that lie is no more protective than a T-shirt on an Arctic glacier. The whole subtext of this place is impermanence and impending doom.

Despite the eternal sunshine,
Every city dweller here knows that
beneath the surface
lurks a slumbering dragon,
which, once woken, will swallow the city, landscape, citizenry in one abysmal gulp. I take comfort knowing that here, death could strike any minute. Apocalypse is no further away than a tick of the clock. Cataclysm loiters on every street corner. I soak in the generosity of the sun, shining as consolation for the perpetually present end.

BETH & SHAWN: I'm happy as a clam. Wish you were here.

MAN WHO SPEAKS SOMEWHERE IN BETWEEN THE SECOND AND THIRD PERSON OMNISCIENT: *(aka* EZRA*)*
Back to the dining hall. Dinner time. Seating arrangement as before. SHAWN. AARON. HENRY. WHACKED OUT ALBANIAN COMPOSER. Tortillas. Peanut butter. Dissonant humming. Chewing.

SHAWN: Thanks for the car.

AARON: You're welcome.

Did you have a good time?

SHAWN: Yeaaaahhhh….

(Pause)

AARON: Do anything…
exciting?

SHAWN: I took a stroll.

AARON: I see.

SHAWN: Down Hollywood Boulevard.

AARON: Really.

SHAWN: Yeah.

Along the Walk of Fame.

HENRY: Walk of Fame, baby.
Aaron, we crack this baby
We'll have a chunk of that sidewalk in no time.

SHAWN: I made notes about the stars along the
sidewalk.
They took up three columns in my notebook.
The first column—
I wrote down all the names I recognized.
The second column—
I wrote down all the names I thought I might recognize
but wasn't sure about.
The third column—
I filled with names no one's ever heard of.

That column goes on and on, page after page after
page….

Scary, don't you think?

(Pause)

Did you make progress today?

HENRY: What the…
Who the fu
Who the hell do you think you are?

AARON: Henry, chill out man, // why are you yelling
at her

HENRY: What did you just say to me Aaron?

AARON: Chill // out

HENRY: Chill Out oh that's just beautiful, Aaron
Chick says "hi" to you
You're ready to like
Throw our whole working relationship down the toilet.
You think I'm gonna let you fuck up my career man
you are //mistaken.

AARON: Come on // Henry

HENRY: Come on Henry *nothing*.
Watch this Aaron:
This is me.
Leaving.

(He storms off. Pause)

SHAWN: Did I
say
something?

AARON: No, he's just…
Whatever.

SHAWN: Wow.
You know…
Aaron…that's your name // right?

AARON: Aaron, // yeah

SHAWN: Aaron

It was
kind of you to
Loan me your car.

AARON: No sweat.

SHAWN: I really liked driving it.

AARON: Cool.

SHAWN: No I mean I really. Really. Liked. Driving it.

AARON: Yeah. I like driving it // too.

SHAWN: I don't know if I should tell you this? but…

AARON: But…what?

SHAWN: I don't know if I should tell you this but
I think you're…
I think you're…

I think you're…

AARON: You think I'm what?

SHAWN: nevermind.

AARON: Okay…
I should uhhh…
Get going.

SHAWN: NO WAIT.

Aaron?

I think you're really
Incredible I think you're
Your car
I think you're
Hhhhhh
Aaron I think you're beautiful and I really want to
have sex with you.

4

WOMAN WHO SPEAKS IN THE SECOND PERSON
OMNISCIENT: *(aka* KATE*)* Now seems like an appropriate
time to segue into scene four.

MAN WHO SPEAKS SOMEWHERE IN BETWEEN THE
SECOND AND THIRD PERSON OMNISCIENT: *(aka* EZRA*)*
The second of five scenes in which Jessica attempts to
reconstruct the contents of her murdered sister's diary.

JESSICA: I've tried to *reconstruct*
I've tried to
Fill in the gaping holes
I've had to
imagine
the contents
of her diary.

WOMAN WHO SPEAKS IN THE SECOND PERSON
OMNISCIENT: *(aka* KATE*)* Listen: Jessica is going to read
her reconstruction of the diary for you.

JESSICA: This first entry I'll share with you was uh
Was written almost exactly a year before my sister was
murdered...

MAN WHO SPEAKS SOMEWHERE IN BETWEEN THE
SECOND AND THIRD PERSON OMNISCIENT: *(aka* EZRA*)*
Somewhere her sister weeps
Tears of frustration and humiliation rain down her face

JESSICA: January 26—Went to Chicago with L for Dad's
annual "Cigar Anointment" Party.
Never again. The whole is event is so medieval and
ridiculous. Boring faculty. *Painfully* boring faculty
spouses, litter of puppy dog grad students salivating
for the prize: the cigar bestowed on them by King
Daddy that will be their ticket into his inner circle. Uch.
If that wasn't enough
L had WAY too much to drink, WAY too early in the
evening.
I wished I'd had a crowbar with me.
To pry Ls nose out of Dad's ass where he'd wedged it
the entire night.
Dad loved it. The more he loved it the deeper L. lodged

it in.
I hate being married sometimes.

WOMAN WHO SPEAKS IN THE SECOND PERSON
OMNISCIENT: *(aka* KATE*)* She watches her husband
Standing next to the fireplace in the living room of
their home
Staring at her silently.

JESSICA: And who was that creature?
My God was that a scene.
Could she have been more blatant?
What was her name? —Syd? Sydney? Shawn?
Schuylar?
I must have blocked it out.
Some boy's name,
There's just about nothing I dislike more than a woman
with a boy's name.
Unbelievable watching whateverhernamewas work the
room.
She will go far, that one.

MAN WHO SPEAKS SOMEWHERE IN BETWEEN THE
SECOND AND THIRD PERSON OMNISCIENT: *(aka* EZRA*)*
Tearing pages from a book
One
By
One.

JESSICA: The thing that really got me
was seeing my father buy into her brilliant little girl
lost routine. L behaved with her exactly the same, no
surprise. He's like a really bad movie sometimes—
know in the first five minutes where the whole thing's
headed. That's the difference between L and Dad. Dad,
predictable as he is, surprises you sometimes—I pretty
much can tell you every word that'll come out of L's
mouth before he says it.

WOMAN WHO SPEAKS IN THE SECOND PERSON
OMNISCIENT: *(aka* KATE*)* And throwing them into the
flames.

JESSICA: It's ridiculous I know—it's been years since
I've even spoken to him, let alone seen him, but…
the more time passes, the more I find myself thinking
about G.

MAN WHO SPEAKS SOMEWHERE IN BETWEEN THE
SECOND AND THIRD PERSON OMNISCIENT: *(aka* EZRA*)*
She watches the paper burn.

JESSICA: Whatever.

Oh, on a less emotionally harrowing note, remember
to clear Wednesday to prepare for Friday's curriculum
review meeting.

5

WOMAN WHO SPEAKS IN THE SECOND PERSON
OMNISCIENT: *(aka* KATE*)* It's the top of scene five and
You're watching the naked bodies of Shawn and Aaron
Sardined precariously on one the twin beds in Shawn's
room.
They stare at the ceiling.
They smoke cigarettes.
They are post-coital.

SHAWN: Fess up, Aaron.
You and your little friend know what I'm working on.
But I don't know a thing about what the two of you are
working on.

AARON: We're writing a screenplay.

SHAWN: That much is obvious. But this screenplay…
Is it some sort of…state secret?
Watching you guys you'd think you were working on
the Manhattan Project.

AARON: Secrecy's important. Can't have people stealing our ideas.

SHAWN: I don't like movies, Aaron.
I haven't been to a movie since my asshole father took me to see *E.T.* when I was eight.
I'm not about to start writing them.

AARON: I really shouldn't talk about it.

WOMAN WHO SPEAKS IN THE SECOND PERSON OMNISCIENT: *(aka* KATE*)* Watch: see Shawn, darting upright?

SHAWN: I just revealed the depths of my sexual soul to you Aaron.
I just exposed to you the frayed nerve that constitutes my entire being
I just reopened for you the festering wound that defines my very existence on this sad and godforsaken planet
And you have the audacity to keep the silly plot of your silly screenplay
you're working on with your silly friend
Secret.
From me.

I could kill you….

AARON: Okay, okay…
It's about a man who brutally murders his wife, then takes his own life.

SHAWN: How daringly original.

AARON: It's based on a true story.

SHAWN: Is it?
Then it must be going swimmingly.

AARON: Actually…we're stuck.
We've been stuck since we got here.

SHAWN: Your friend does seem like a real dick.

AARON: All that crap in the brochure about providing artists a place for contemplation, regeneration, cross-pollination?

SHAWN: Fornication?

AARON: They didn't mention *stagnation.*

SHAWN: Could it be your idea is what's stagnant?

AARON: No no no
It's an incredible story.

SHAWN: Pray tell.

AARON: Married couple. Young, attractive, successful

SHAWN: Okay…

AARON: Seeming poster children for the modern successful marriage. What's more, the wife is three months pregnant.

SHAWN: I'm hanging on the edge of my seat.

AARON: But festering underneath this perfect marriage, is a tangled web of lies, secrets, denial.

SHAWN: Your originality is truly staggering.

AARON: It's based on a true story.

SHAWN: Yes, you said that before.

AARON: Happened about five years ago. It was huge. It was all over the newspapers.

SHAWN: I don't understand. With all that newsprint lining kitty litter boxes across the nation
How on earth could you possibly be stuck?

AARON: Too many holes.
Too many unanswered questions.

SHAWN: Like?

AARON: For one, the big "why?" question.

SHAWN: That's a scary question.

AARON: Why. Why. Why. Why did it happen? What set the wheels in motion in the first place.
I mean this couple: last people on earth you'd think would end up murder-suicides

SHAWN: Pray tell, Aaron:
Whose ass isn't up for grabs in the new millennium?

AARON: And where it happens: last place you'd imagine
Small, quiet, upper middle class college town in Massachusetts

SHAWN: Hm.

AARON: The murder victim was the daughter of a prominent academic.

WOMAN WHO SPEAKS IN THE THIRD PERSON OMNISCIENT: *(aka* KATE*)* Hear the long pause? Watch Shawn as she slowly lays back, head sharing the pillow with Aaron.

SHAWN: I knew there must've been a reason for my otherwise inexplicable attraction to you.

AARON: What does that mean?

SHAWN: This academic. He wasn't…
By chance…
Affiliated with the University of Chicago.

AARON: So you do know the story.

SHAWN: Oh boy do I know the story.

AARON: I knew you had to have seen it on the news.

SHAWN: Oh I didn't need the news to know that story.

AARON: Meaning….

SHAWN: The year before this murder of yours? I won the cigar.

AARON: Huh?

SHAWN: This academic of yours?
He anointed me with it.

AARON: Pardon me?

SHAWN: I was his protégé.

WOMAN WHO SPEAKS IN THE THIRD PERSON
OMNISCIENT: *(aka* KATE*)* Did you just see Aaron shoot
up to his knees upon hearing that tidbit of information?

AARON: YOU WERE WHAT?!?!?!?!

SHAWN: Once upon a time
I was a first year graduate student.
Fall of that year I wrote a paper.
About a certain magician.
A paper so outstanding
I won the cigar that year.

AARON: Wait a second you lost me on this cigar thing.

SHAWN: Each year Oscar

AARON: Holy shit you know // his name

SHAWN: Each year *Oscar* would throw a lavish party—
Well…in truth his *wife* threw it
but let's not split hairs.

At this party
Oscar would award a cigar
to his most promising first year.
And that year,
His most promising first year,
Was *me*.

AARON: Whoa.

SHAWN: He became my mentor.
I became his *protégé.*

He's the reason
I'm writing
my book.

AARON: Wait a minute: are you telling me—

SHAWN: That Oscar and I were also lovers?

AARON: Holy
fucking
shit…

SHAWN: I think you know the answer without me
telling you.

Where are you going?

WOMAN WHO SPEAKS IN THE THIRD PERSON
OMNISCIENT: *(aka* KATE*)* Did you just see Aaron shoot
up to his feet, and dash out of the room, jockey shorts
in hand?

SHAWN: Don't go. Please? Don't go.

6

WOMAN WHO SPEAKS IN THE SECOND PERSON
OMNISCIENT: *(aka* KATE*)* Now seems like an appropriate
time to segue into scene six.

MAN WHO SPEAKS SOMEWHERE IN BETWEEN THE
SECOND AND THIRD PERSON OMNISCIENT: *(aka* EZRA*)*
The third of five scenes in which Jessica attempts to
reconstruct the contents of her murdered sister's diary.

JESSICA: I've tried to *reconstruct*
I've tried to
Fill in the gaping holes
I've had to
imagine
the contents
of my sister's diary.

WOMAN WHO SPEAKS IN THE SECOND PERSON
OMNISCIENT: *(aka* KATE*)* Listen: Jessica is going to read
her reconstruction of the diary for you.

JESSICA: No one in my family knew my sister was
pregnant when she was murdered.
Another shocker. She was ambivalent about children.
Especially at that particular stage of her career.
When the coroner's report came back saying she was
three months pregnant…
I

MAN WHO SPEAKS SOMEWHERE IN BETWEEN THE
SECOND AND THIRD PERSON OMNISCIENT: *(aka* EZRA*)*
Somewhere her sister weeps.
Tears of frustration and humiliation rain down her
face.

WOMAN WHO SPEAKS IN THE SECOND PERSON
OMNISCIENT: *(aka* KATE*)* She watches her husband
Standing next to the fireplace in the living room of
their home
Staring at her silently.

JESSICA: I couldn't make out the date on this entry but
It's safe to assume
she wrote it a
Month? Month and a half?
Before she was murdered.

MAN WHO SPEAKS SOMEWHERE IN BETWEEN THE
SECOND AND THIRD PERSON OMNISCIENT: *(aka* EZRA*)*
Tearing pages from a book
One
By
One.

WOMAN WHO SPEAKS IN THE SECOND PERSON
OMNISCIENT: *(aka* KATE*)* And throwing them into the
flames.

MAN WHO SPEAKS SOMEWHERE IN BETWEEN THE
SECOND AND THIRD PERSON OMNISCIENT: *(aka* EZRA*)*
She watches the paper burn.

JESSICA: She wrote:

To keep
Or not to keep.

Listen to yourself.
"Not to keep."
As if it were something I could just
Drop off at the Salvation Army.

Let's not mince words. Girl: you are in serious shit.

Let me rephrase the question:
To keep
Or to rid myself of it.

That's more like it.
Sends my stomach into a free fall,
But it's the truth.
Much as I'd like to detach myself.
Much as I'd like to be glib about the whole thing.

Let's talk options, shall we?

Option 1:
Have it.
Hope that by having it L & I can go back to what it was
like before.
Undo the sham of everything.
Problem with option 1: wishful thinking.

Option 2:
Have it.
Knowing that it won't change a thing.
Ride out the sham of everything.
Problem with option 2: Secrets, and more secrets,
growing deeper, darker. Living hell.

Option 3:
Have it.
But only after I leave.
Which means I'd have to leave soon.
Not a secret you can keep for long.

Problem with option 3: where to go? What to do when I get there? I love my job. Besides, L's not one to let go of things. Living hell.

Option 4:
Get rid of it and never tell.
Problem with option 4: Can I live with that kind of secret?

Option 5:
Get rid of it and tell.
Problem with option 5: Can you spell the end of everything?

Option 6:
Maybe my body will make that decision for me again. Problem with option 6: Though in that respect, my body's been pretty reliable before, this is something I can't count on. You can't forget the depression after the other times. I almost didn't come out of it last time. It can only get worse.

WOMAN WHO SPEAKS IN THE SECOND PERSON OMNISCIENT: *(aka* KATE*)* Now might be a good time to take a ten minute intermission.

END OF ACT ONE

ACT TWO

7

WOMAN WHO SPEAKS IN THE SECOND PERSON OMNISCIENT: *(aka* KATE*)* Welcome back. You just missed Aaron charge into Henry's room, half dressed, hair disheveled, carrying with him the strong scent of Shawn. If you hurry up you'll catch scene seven in progress:

HENRY: HOLY SHIT!

AARON: I'm telling you, she knew the whole family. Oscar. Marisol. Their daughters.

HENRY: HOLY SHIT!

AARON: She was his protégé.

HENRY: HOLY SHIT!

AARON: They were having an affair while she was writing her dissertation.

HENRY: Aaron…

AARON: That's why she's here writing her book.

HENRY: Aaron…

AARON: To put the whole thing behind her.

HENRY: Aaron…oh Aaron

WOMAN WHO SPEAKS IN THE SECOND PERSON OMNISCIENT: *(aka* KATE*)* Witness: a genuine moment of affection between two heterosexual men. Henry bear hugging and cheek kissing Aaron like a vodka-juiced Russian.

HENRY: Dude: I am so sorry I dissed you before.

AARON: Don't sweat it H-bomb.

HENRY: Let's get to work.

WOMAN WHO SPEAKS IN THE SECOND PERSON OMNISCIENT: *(aka* KATE*)* Witness: half-clothed, disheveled Aaron takes his seat behind the laptop. Henry lights a cigarette, paces. As they write, the scent of Shawn imperceptibly fades from the room.

HENRY: Okay. We're in one of the ramshackle dorm rooms of the artist's colony.

AARON: You're not supposed to smoke in here.

HENRY: And it's like
The longest room in the world

AARON: Management's gonna kick us out.

HENRY: It goes on for like
Forever
Like the hotel hallway at the beginning of that Pink Floyd movie….

AARON: Look, dude

Nina'll be pissed if I come home clothes smelling like smoke
She'll think I took it up again.

HENRY: Only it's not a hallway but the dorm room

AARON: Hey are you listening to me?

HENRY: Yeah yeah smoke Nina smell one more drag I'll put it out.

(Sucks in a big inhale, jabs the cigarette out)

See?

(Exhale)

Okay.
Point of view: Few inches above the floor
We move through a canyon of
Twin beds
Twin bed after twin bed
Slowly
Until we reach the last bed
The camera slowly rises to an overhead shot of Shawn
lying on the bed
Should she be naked?

AARON: No. Not yet. I see her more in
Like an old t-shirt, ratty sweat pants.

HENRY: Okay:
Overhead shot of Shawn
Staring up at the *ceiling.*
Chestnut hair wild, spread out over the pillow.
She's pale.
Faraway look in her eyes.
Arms tangled around her head.
In her left hand
A little black tape recorder.

AARON: Rigor mortis moment

HENRY: Riggamortiwhat?

AARON: Rigor mortis moment:
Swift, mechanical move,
she swings the tape recorder to her mouth—

HENRY: clicks the record button soon as it gets to her
lips.
She speaks.
Unnerving monotone.

SHAWN: Chapter Seven
"Bullet Through a Disguise
(colon)

(subtitle)
Chung Ling Soo and the Bullet Catch Effect"

HENRY: See:
Shawn's totally immersed in writing chapter seven.
Totally immersed in the biography of

SHAWN: Chung Ling Soo, Marvelous Chinese Conjurer.

HENRY: And his fateful attempt at the Bullet Catch
Effect.

SHAWN: Thing is, he wasn't really Chinese.
He only pretended he was Chinese

HENRY: Shawn's totally immersed in the chapter—
she's no longer the cool, clinical academic in dealing
with her subject. Voice over:

SHAWN: Seems like I'm no longer writing something
outside of myself.

Seems like I just dove head first into my narrative.

AARON: Oooooh!

HENRY: What?

AARON: Montage time.

HENRY: Talk to me Aaron.

AARON: Intercut images in Shawn's voice over with
images from the Cigar Party.

HENRY: What are you talking about?

AARON: Trust me.

HENRY: Fine: We hear Shawn's voice over—Montage

SHAWN: I'm on stage wearing the skimpy costume of
Chung Ling Soo's assistant. The shoes don't fit right,
as this is ordinarily not my role. The woman usually
playing it is Chung's wife.

AARON: Shot of Marisol's shoes. Same color. She makes
final preparations for the Cigar Party.

HENRY: Awesome. Even if I have no idea what you're talking about.

SHAWN: Chung's wife is the only one he trusts with the secrets behind his magic.

AARON: Marisol inspects the flower arrangements, the banquet spread.

Checks her makeup and hair in the mirror

SHAWN: Seems the fact that Chung and I are having an affair has taken its toll on her nerves. I'm substituting for her while she convalesces.

AARON: Quick shot of Marisol impaling a blood red apple in a roasted pig's mouth.

SHAWN: This night—March 23, 1918—we perform at the Wood Green Empire Theatre in London. While the country suffers war fatigue, the audience, on the edge of its seats, wait to witness the final, death defying feat of the night: Soo's Bullet Catch Effect.

AARON: Party arrivals. Faculty, faculty spouses….

HENRY: Cocktails, wine, champagne, hors d'oeurves.

AARON: Grad students antsy for the big event: the Cigar Anointment Ritual.

HENRY: We gotta get murdered daughter in somehow

AARON: Right…what about this. Doorbell rings, murdered daughter, husband arrive. Murdered daughter notices: lurking in the shadows, talking to Oscar,

AARON & HENRY: Shawn.

SHAWN: So far, the show has gone off without a hitch. I'm already thinking about *after* the show. The celebration. The elite of London toasting us.

AARON: Moment of truth. Oscar raps his fork against his champagne flute, commanding the obedience of his guests.

HENRY: Room goes silent.

SHAWN: At the celebration Chung will have to continue his Chinaman performance, the silent bows, the Cantonese sounding gibberish, maintaining the illusion he can't speak a word of English, sustaining the aura of mystery to keep the world believing.

AARON: Ritual's about to begin. Oscar removes the most expensive cigar from his humidor.

HENRY: Genuine Cohiba, baby.

SHAWN: The music swells. Gongs crash, Smoke fills the stage. Soo, in spectacular satin robes, appears seated peacefully on a gaudy faux-Ming-era throne while I prepare the rifle.

AARON: Oscar begins his speech.

HENRY: What's he say?

AARON: We'll worry about the dialogue later.

SHAWN: I invite on stage a soldier—to authenticate my weapon and the round of ammunition I insert into the barrel. I make this encounter as erotic as permissible.

AARON: Speech continues. Laughter. Anticipation. Applause.

SHAWN: I invite on stage an upper class, middle aged woman to inspect the inside of Chung's mouth with her finger to verify nothing is hidden under his tongue—

AARON: Speech ends. Moment of truth arrives. Oscar's about to award the cigar.

SHAWN: When we're alone again I aim the rifle at Chung across the stage.
An imperceptible nod from him, I know he's ready.

AARON: Oscar mouths a name.

HENRY: Shawn's name.

SHAWN: The music crescendos, followed by silence save the low rumble of timpani.

AARON: Polite, slightly awkward applause tinged with envy.

SHAWN: My finger is on the trigger.
I focus on the rifle sight.

AARON: And the moment: Oscar hands Shawn the cigar

SHAWN: I exert pressure on my finger.

AARON: He doesn't expect she'll smoke it, but
She inserts it in her mouth like a dare
throwing the unflappable Oscar for a loop.

SHAWN: I squeeze the trigger.

HENRY: He fumbles for his Zippo
Manages to conjure up a flame

AARON: And lights the tip of her cigar.

SHAWN: I hear an explosion. Loud, Like an artillery shell.

HENRY: A veil of smoke

AARON: They stare at each other knowingly.

SHAWN: And time stops.

(Pause)

HENRY: Aaron?

AARON: Yeah?

HENRY: This shit really burns and all but

AARON: But what?

HENRY: What does any of this have to do with the murder?

(Pause)

AARON: I don't know.

WOMAN WHO SPEAKS IN THE SECOND PERSON OMNISCIENT: *(aka* BETH) Listen:
Hear them silent as the clock ticks...ticks...ticks...?

AARON: oooohhhhh
I think I got it:

HENRY: Hit me.

AARON: ...Closeup of Murdered Daughter's eyes.

HENRY: Okay...

AARON: We uhh....
see the moment from Murdered Daughter's P OV.

HENRY: Okay...?

AARON: She sees...
Shawn: lit Cohiba wedged between her full, red lips...

HENRY: And?

AARON: I don't know...
Shawn's *naked.*

HENRY: Awesome.

AARON: She's naked and her...
Her body's wedged, undulating between Oscar
and his son in law

HENRY: Slow down there cowboy.

AARON: Clothed, Henry. The guys are clothed.

HENRY: Alright, cool.

AARON: *That's.* what Murdered Daughter sees:
Shawn, lit Cohiba between her lips,

Naked
Undulating between Oscar and his son-in-law—
Murdered Daughter's. husband.
Fully clothed,
Also smoking cigars.

HENRY: You're a fucking genius.

AARON: Okay. End of montage.
CUT TO: Close up of the rifle barrel opening.
We're in super slow motion.

HENRY: The bullet slowly exits the sheath of the rifle.
Sound of the report mangled, distorted.

AARON: CUT TO: reverse angle. Above and behind the bullet
as we trail its slow progress across the stage towards Chung

HENRY: CUT TO Brits in the audience gaping in awe.

AARON: CUT TO close up of Chung. His face, his fake Chinese mask an advertisement for Taoist placidity.

HENRY: CUT TO the bullet, making its slow, steady progress across the stage.

AARON: CUT TO: close up of Shawn,
As Chung's scantily clad assistant,
Something about her face seems wrong. Puzzled.

HENRY: Like she senses a catastrophe in the making.

AARON: Like she knows this point will mark forever a before and after in her life.

HENRY: CUT TO: closeup profile of Chung,

AARON: Only it's NOT Chung's face

AARON & HENRY: IT'S OSCAR'S FACE

HENRY: Oh, baby.

AARON: mouth open slightly, still peaceful, blissfully unaware that he, his assistant, and every man woman and child watching has crossed an indelible line in time. The line separating the before and the after.

HENRY: The bullet enters the frame, headed for his top row of teeth.

SHAWN: Strange…

From where I stand
His lips seem to expand
Almost imperceptibly.
At first I think I'm seeing things,
But his lips keep growing,
until his mouth becomes a wound that takes up half his face.

Then I hear him yell
In perfect English:
"My God I've been shot. Close the curtain…."

(She clicks off the recorder.)

In that moment…
he totally destroyed the illusion.

HENRY: Okay.
She clicks off the recorder, reverse riggawhatever,
Same shot as the top of the scene.
Shawn. Staring up at the ceiling. Hair wild. Faraway look in her eyes.

Then imperceptibly.
The camera slowly corckscrews down
In the direction of Shawn's *eyes*
"Black, like a doll's eyes"
Closer and closer
Until we freefall into her retina.

AARON: That's great.

HENRY: No, fuck it. We already did that in the last one.

AARON: Yeah, but the last one never got made.

HENRY: But this one *will* get made
And when *this* one gets made
Everyone will want to make the *last* one.

AARON: Dude, that's just your mimesophobia
speaking.

HENRY: My mimesowhat?

AARON: Mimesophobia.

HENRY: Help me out here Aaron I'm not the one who
graduated magna cum laude from Yale.

AARON: Mimesophobia. Means the morbid fear of
slavish imitation.

(Pause)

HENRY: Is it dinnertime yet?

8

WOMAN WHO SPEAKS IN THE SECOND PERSON
OMNISCIENT: *(aka* KATE*)* Now seems like an appropriate
time to segue into scene eight.

MAN WHO SPEAKS SOMEWHERE IN BETWEEN THE
SECOND AND THIRD PERSON OMNISCIENT: *(aka* EZRA*)*
The fourth of five scenes in which Jessica attempts to
reconstruct the contents of her murdered sister's diary.

JESSICA: I've tried to *reconstruct*
I've tried to
Fill in the gaping holes
I've had to
imagine
the contents
of my late sister's diary.

WOMAN WHO SPEAKS IN THE SECOND PERSON
OMNISCIENT: *(aka* KATE*)* Listen: Jessica is going to read
her reconstruction of the diary for you.

JESSICA: This last entry I'll uhh
share with you was
Was the most difficult to reconstruct because…
Well

It was the one she was
Clutching.
In her hands.
When they
found her body.
It was….
It was crumpled.
Covered in her…

In my sister's blood.

MAN WHO SPEAKS SOMEWHERE IN BETWEEN THE
SECOND AND THIRD PERSON OMNISCIENT: *(aka* EZRA*)*
Somewhere her sister weeps
Tears of frustration and humiliation rain down her
face.

WOMAN WHO SPEAKS IN THE SECOND PERSON
OMNISCIENT: *(aka* KATE*)* She watches her husband
Next to the fireplace in the living room of their home
Staring at her silently

MAN WHO SPEAKS SOMEWHERE IN BETWEEN THE
SECOND AND THIRD PERSON OMNISCIENT: *(aka* EZRA*)*
Tearing pages from a book
One
By
One.

WOMAN WHO SPEAKS IN THE SECOND PERSON
OMNISCIENT: *(aka* KATE*)* And throwing them into the
flames.

JESSICA: This is what she wrote:

Confession time.
Called G today.

Googled his number.
203 area code.
Turns out he lives in New Haven.

So stupid.
Like a teenager.
I must have dialed the number ten times
Always hanging up before punching in the last
number.
Finally mustered up the nerve to dial the whole thing.

I felt like my heart was going to explode while the
phone rang
I hoped he wouldn't answer
that I could leave a message
put the burden on him to call back

But he picked up the phone.
It's been what? Eight years?
But his voice on the other end of the line.
Familiar.
As if no time had passed.
"Hello," he said.

MAN WHO SPEAKS SOMEWHERE IN BETWEEN THE
SECOND AND THIRD PERSON OMNISCIENT: (aka EZRA)
Somewhere her sister weeps
Tears of frustration and humiliation rain down her face

JESSICA: There was an awkward pause, I said…
"Hi."
That's all I needed to say.
He knew exactly who I was
Like he was expecting my call.
After eight
Years.

WOMAN WHO SPEAKS IN THE SECOND PERSON
OMNISCIENT: (aka KATE) She watches her husband
Standing next to the fireplace in the living room of

their home
Staring at her silently

JESSICA: It's insane, I know. But…
we made plans.
We're
meeting for dinner Monday night in New Haven.

MAN WHO SPEAKS SOMEWHERE IN BETWEEN THE
SECOND AND THIRD PERSON OMNISCIENT: *(aka* EZRA*)*
Tearing pages from a book
One
By
One.
And throwing them into the flames.

JESSICA: Talking to him I remember…
I remember what it's like
To be
heard.

MAN WHO SPEAKS SOMEWHERE IN BETWEEN THE
SECOND AND THIRD PERSON OMNISCIENT: *(aka* EZRA*)*
He tosses the binding of the diary into the fire.

WOMAN WHO SPEAKS IN THE SECOND PERSON
OMNISCIENT: *(aka* KATE*)* The binding takes a little
longer than the diary's pages to turn into ash.

JESSICA: God.

The sham of everything.

9

MAN WHO SPEAKS SOMEWHERE IN BETWEEN THE
SECOND AND THIRD PERSON OMNISCIENT: *(aka* EZRA*)*
Watch: Breakfast at the colony the morning after
HENRY and AARON's creative super nova. Note
the haggard buzz in their eyes. They shovel food into
their mouths from their starch and protein saturated

breakfast plates, as they try to sustain their fourth wind after a sleepless night of feverish screenwriting.

They write while they eat, AARON typing on the laptop, HENRY struggling to regulate the pace of his chewing with the kaleidoscope of images that pour out his mouth. They're nearing the end of their screenplay.

Also at the table, the WHACKED OUT ALBANIAN COMPOSER. Humming all dissonant while chewing real loud. As the scene progresses, the humming and chewing evolve from random, nerve-grating noise to near perfect underscoring of the images conjured by HENRY and AARON.

The seat normally occupied by SHAWN? Empty.

Tortillas and peanut butter? Nowhere to be seen.

HENRY and AARON don't notice her absence.

Let's check in, see how things are going.

Hi guys.

AARON & HENRY: Hey.

MAN WHO SPEAKS SOMEWHERE IN BETWEEN THE SECOND AND THIRD PERSON OMNISCIENT: *(aka EZRA)* How's the ol' screenplay going?

AARON: Great. // Awesome

HENRY: Yeah, dude, don't stand too close, you might catch fire.

MAN WHO SPEAKS SOMEWHERE IN BETWEEN THE SECOND AND THIRD PERSON OMNISCIENT: *(aka EZRA)* I was going to say...you guys look pretty—

HENRY: Wired? Dude: we've been up like I don't know how many hours straight. Feels like morning seven of a weeklong crystal meth binge.

MAN WHO SPEAKS SOMEWHERE IN BETWEEN THE SECOND AND THIRD PERSON OMNISCIENT: *(aka EZRA)*

I see. So it's safe to say the uhh…the colony is working out for you.

HENRY: All I can say dude? first two weeks here I thought this place sucks bunch of frickin' weirdoes runnin' around crappy food crappy rooms just banging our heads against the wall I mean I was ready eat Drano get it over with you know what I'm saying? going fucking stir crazy trying to find the hook know what I'm saying? the *hook* the *hook* the *hook* where's the *hook* the *in* the *penny drop moment* the *Rosebud* crazy thing is the *hook* was staring us in the face the whole time from the word go and granted if it wasn't for my partner here my buddy my new hero Dirk Diggler over here's suavity we'd still be sitting around staring at the wallpaper tugging on our pubic hair wishing we were dead

AARON: That's gross Henry.

HENRY: Sorry, dude. But to answer your question: what was your question?

MAN WHO SPEAKS SOMEWHERE IN BETWEEN THE SECOND AND THIRD PERSON OMNISCIENT: *(aka* EZRA*)* The colony…it's worked out for // you

HENRY: Yeah yeah yeah yeah if the guys who run this place ever need a testimonial? sign me up.

MAN WHO SPEAKS SOMEWHERE IN BETWEEN THE SECOND AND THIRD PERSON OMNISCIENT: *(aka* EZRA*)* So, I take it you found your… *hook.*

HENRY: Oh we found it. Its more than a hook it's a left hook a right hook another right a jab a jab an uppercut a jab he's hurting oh you can see him up against the ropes then BOOM monster right hook and he's down on the canvas for the count.

Man Who Speaks Somewhere In Between The
Second And Third Person Omniscient: *(aka* Ezra*)*
I see. Care to…share with us this… *hook?*

Henry: No can do, dude. Sworn to secrecy til the
movie's in the can.

Man Who Speaks Somewhere In Between The
Second And Third Person Omniscient: *(aka* Ezra*)*
Um. I hate to rain on your parade but…
the movie already came out.

Henry: What?

Man Who Speaks Somewhere In Between The
Second And Third Person Omniscient: *(aka* Ezra*)*
It's huge. Monster hit. There's even Oscar buzz.

Henry: How is that possible?

Aaron: Yeah, we haven't even finished the script.

Man Who Speaks Somewhere In Between The
Second And Third Person Omniscient: *(aka* Ezra*)*
Guys: You're not the real Henry and Aaron.
Remember? This is a reenactment?

Henry: Oh.

Aaron: Right. Does that mean Shawn and I didn't…

Man Who Speaks Somewhere In Between The
Second And Third Person Omniscient: *(aka* Ezra*)*
Sorry.

Aaron: Oh.

Man Who Speaks Somewhere In Between The
Second And Third Person Omniscient: *(aka* Ezra*)*
So given that the movie's already a smash, maybe you
could
Give us a little insight into this
Hook.

HENRY: Okay: goes something like this:
We got Oscar—hugely famous academic—

AARON: Famous in academic circles—not famous like
movie star famous.

HENRY: Right.

Oscar, Marisol, their two daughters.
All indications, family's a picture of perfection,
Well-educated, wealthy, ambitious, brilliant, attractive,
amazingly accomplished.
Enter Shawn,
Oscar's new protégé—
She's also totally brilliant

AARON: But she's got an unstable streak.

HENRY: Oscar takes her under his wing. Partly cause
she's brilliant.
Partly cause she's totally hot.

AARON: And partly because she's a little nuts.

HENRY: That's right—Oscar's a risk-taker—
How else did he get to be in his position in the first
place.
And so, not only is she his protégé,
Not only does he take her into the family—

AARON: Her own family's an embarrassment to her—

HENRY: He's also banging her.
And not only is *he* banging her, turns out
His *son-in-law* is banging her too. Twisted family
menage
And it's not like anyone being subtle about it,
They're practically rubbing it in everyone's faces,

AARON: Especially Murdered Daughter's face.

HENRY: *Especially* way she finds out—just so happens
she stumbles on a videotape—
crude, homemade job of Shawn, son-in-law *and* Oscar

tangled up in a three-way
wearing plastic pig Halloween masks.

AARON: I don't know Henry, I'm a little iffy about that
sequence.

HENRY: Anyway—Threesome or no threesome,
Murdered Daughter's none too happy about this.
So what does she do? She seeks comfort, runs into the
arms of her college sweetheart—

AARON: He's the one that got away. Oposite of the rest
of her family. Uncomplicated. Laid back.

HENRY: Kind of guy who sells incense, wampum the
latest in hemp fashion in Vermont.

AARON: Meanwhile, Shawn's star is on the rise.

HENRY: She's getting cigars left and right from all kinds
of people

AARON: Both in *and* out of the academy

HENRY: Which cools Oscar to her. He's threatened by
her success.
He starts to disassociate himself from Shawn,
starts to cut into her, you know what I'm saying? and
Shawn...
What's the saying?

AARON: "Hell hath no fury like a woman scorned."

HENRY: That's right. Shawn, through a series of
coincidences,

AARON: Which we're still working out—

HENRY: figures out Murdered Daughter's been banging
an old college beau.
So what does Shawn do? After a steamy session with
son-in-law
she lets slip this little fact.
Turns out, this tidbit coincides with son-in-law having
just learned his wife's pregnant

AARON: So naturally he gets suspicious.

HENRY: He has her followed.
Installs Spyware on her computer.
Reads her diary,
Becomes convinced the kid's not his.
He goes ballistic.
Does a number on her,
Does a number on himself.
And Shawn
In a final attempt to break free of Oscar,
Goes off and writes her book.
When it comes out it's huge.
Her star rises to heights only dreamed of by Oscar.
Oscar's crushed with guilt.
Family falls apart
Shawn gets away with murder.
End of story.

AARON: Well, almost…there's a few threads that need tying up.

MAN WHO SPEAKS SOMEWHERE IN BETWEEN THE SECOND AND THIRD PERSON OMNISCIENT: *(aka* EZRA*)* So *Shawn's* the hook.

HENRY: That's right.

MAN WHO SPEAKS SOMEWHERE IN BETWEEN THE SECOND AND THIRD PERSON OMNISCIENT: *(aka* EZRA*)* But Shawn never finished her book.

HENRY: What?

AARON: Yeah…where is Shawn, anyway?

MAN WHO SPEAKS SOMEWHERE IN BETWEEN THE SECOND AND THIRD PERSON OMNISCIENT: *(aka* EZRA*)* Watch: HENRY and AARON notice for the first time the seat at the table normally occupied by SHAWN is empty. Note: The foreboding silence in which HENRY and AARON conceal their sudden doubts about the

foundation and plausibility of their premise. Listen:
Henry breaks the silence before such doubts can knock
down their narrative house of cards.

HENRY: Look, we're in the middle of getting to the
end—you mind…?

MAN WHO SPEAKS SOMEWHERE IN BETWEEN THE
SECOND AND THIRD PERSON OMNISCIENT: *(aka* EZRA*)*
Of course, by all means.

HENRY: Okay. Penultimate scene.

MAN WHO SPEAKS SOMEWHERE IN BETWEEN THE
SECOND AND THIRD PERSON OMNISCIENT: *(aka* EZRA*)*
While Henry and Aaron careen towards the end
of their movie, let's check in upstairs, see what's
happening in Shawn's world. Kate?

WOMAN WHO SPEAKS IN THE SECOND PERSON
OMNISCIENT: *(aka* KATE*)* Thanks, Ezra.
We're standing outside Shawn's dorm room at the
colony.
The door is locked.
While we can't see her, we can imagine she's teetering
at a precipice.

SHAWN: *(Talking into the tape recorder)*
Here's what I see when I tilt my head
My breasts underneath the old t-shirt I wear
My bare feet
My toes
The room is long and narrow
Rotting green wallpaper,
Line of twin beds just like mine
Wooden door at the end of the room.
Closed.
Light through the slit at the bottom of the door.

MAN WHO SPEAKS SOMEWHERE IN BETWEEN THE
SECOND AND THIRD PERSON OMNISCIENT: *(aka* EZRA*)*

In an amazing display of psychic cross-pollination,
Henry dictates images of Shawn uncannily similar to
what's happening upstairs in her room.

HENRY: Okay. She's lying on the bed,
Looking at the door, far end of the room.
Suddenly // the room telescopes outward.

SHAWN: Suddenly, the room telescopes outward
Longer and longer
Doorway growing smaller and smaller
Until it's the size of a postage stamp.

HENRY:	SHAWN:
She gets to her feet	I get to my feet

SHAWN: I collapse onto the ground
// And crawl.

HENRY: She crawls towards the door

SHAWN: Every inch I crawl
The door gets further away

HENRY: She crawls faster
Hands and knees bloody from the crawling

SHAWN: I'm so close I can almost touch it

HENRY: Finally she reaches the door.
Shadows of monsters and the knees of small children
Flicker in the light through the slit at the bottom of the
door

SHAWN: I reach the door. Exhausted.
// And in my exhaustion I lean against it.

HENRY: She's exhausted
She leans against the door with her shoulder…

SHAWN: Suddenly I can see it…a blaze of light:
The keystone
The magic shard of kryptonite
The cat burglar's pick that once turned will….
I reach for a blank legal pad and pen.

My pen moves on autopilot
filling line after line page after page legal pad after
blank legal pad
As I write I hear the cat burglar's sweet music
The sweet and resonant ching of tumblers // falling...

HENRY: Suddenly, the door opens

Shawn finds herself blinded by television studio lights,
moments before this evening's broadcast of Charlie
Rose. She's at the table in Charlie's Den of Starfucking
sitting across from Charlie Rose himself, cheeks ruddy
like a freshly spanked baby's behind.

MAN WHO SPEAKS SOMEWHERE IN BETWEEN THE
SECOND AND THIRD PERSON OMNISCIENT: (aka EZRA)
As they flesh out this sequence, it crosses neither
Henry nor Aaron's mind to make note of the eerie
scratching noises coming from the direction of Shawn's
room.

HENRY: What's she wearing?

AARON: Who gives a shit what she's wearing?

HENRY: It's gotta be something
I don't know
Something...
that reflects who she is

(Pause)

AARON: I think of her kind of like
if you fused Hanna Arendt with Nicole Kidman
High power intellectual glommed with Hollywood
Diva
Mountain of credit card debt

HENRY: Trust fund?

AARON: No. Self made. More empathetic that way.

HENRY: What do I know about clothes?
Hey, why don't you call Nina?

AARON: You call Nina.

HENRY: Riiiight.
(He pulls out his cell phone. Dials)
I love this thing. You can be at the ass end of the
universe and still get a signal. One time I was up on a
volcano in Hawai—
Nina.
Hey, it's me. Henry.
Yeah, we're up here. It's going great. Little weird
sometimes, but great.
Listen: Aaron would've called but uh
he just stepped out for a smoke.

AARON: You // dick

HENRY: We've got a female question.
Imagine you were like
Some hot academic
U Chicago type
You've just written a book, "think piece" that's all the
buzz
Best seller—not number one—more like number
twelve
You're young.
Couple of years out of grad school.
You're brash.
You're a little nutty but in a totally sexy way.
Way Aaron and I describe her she's like
If Nicole Kidman and….

AARON: *Hanna Are//ndt*

HENRY: Hanna Aren't got together and had a demon
child.
Also, she lives like
Way beyond her means.
Get the picture?
Anyway, who invites you on their show
But none other than Charlie Rose. What would you

wear?
Oh. Good question.
*Aaron: Is she the guest for the full hour, half hour or filler for
the last ten minutes?*

AARON: *Raise the stakes man, she's on for the hour.*

HENRY: Hour.
Okay.
Skirt or pants?
Pants. Really. Okay:
Gucci suit. Black. Same cut as the one Nicole Kidman
wore to the Golden Globes.
Low what?
Spell that for me?
Aaron: Low decollatege d-e-c-o-l-l-a-t-e-g-e.
Shoes?
Manolo Blahnik... How do you spell that?

AARON: I know how to spell it.

HENRY: Really?
You think what, red?
Nude. Hm.
Aaron: nude Manolo Blahnik's
Now hair and eyewear.
From the neck up she's more the Hannah Aren't beat.
Brown hair.
Chopsticks. Great idea.
*Aaron: hair in a bun, held in place by two chopsticks,
Vintage cat's eye glasses.*
Nina, you're a genius.
Yeah, I gotta go and write this thing now.
Next Saturday? Yeah, count me in.
Alright.
Alright.
Alright.
No shit.
Alright.

Alright.
Yeah, I'll have Aaron call you later.
Okay, bye.

AARON: You're a dick.

HENRY: Alright, what happens next.

AARON: Final sequence.

HENRY: Whatchya got for me?

AARON: Studio. Shawn across from Charlie Rose.
We hear the jazz that signifies the beginning of the broadcast.
We pan from the desk in the direction of the studio camera—
Which stares back at us like a robot Cyclops,
Black except for the faint reflection of Shawn and Charlie.
We zoom into it, disappear into blackness.
We shift into high speed,
Racing through a labyrinth of fiber optic cables,
Until we're launched out from a massive satellite dish.
We hear a huge whoosh
Landscape of New York City shrinks below as we power through the atmosphere
Into outer space.
We reach a satellite, which deflects us, beams us back down to earth. We freefall towards a bright speck on the shore of Lake Michigan. As we get closer we see the cityscape of Chicago, closer and closer until we reach the heart of Hyde Park….

HENRY: CUT TO

Exterior. OSCAR and MARISOL's prairie style house in Hyde Park, Chicago. January. Night.
The windows are dark. We track towards the house, towards one of the windows, closer and closer until we pass through // it….

Man Who Speaks Somewhere In Between The
Second And Third Person Omniscient: *(aka* Ezra*)*
While Henry and Aaron compose the final sequence
of the film—the same sequence you saw way back
when during the Prologue—the scratching sounds
coming from Shawn's room grow more and more
present. Henry and Aaron, seeing the light at the end
of the tunnel, don't notice. Tell you what: let's see what
Beth, Shawn's mother can tell us about what exactly
happened up in her daughter's room. Kate?

Woman Who Speaks In The Second Person
Omniscient: *(aka* Kate*)* Yes, Ezra.

Man Who Speaks Somewhere In Between The
Second And Third Person Omniscient: *(aka* Ezra*)*
Would you mind being Beth for one last time?

Woman Who Speaks In The Second Person
Omniscient: *(aka* Kate*)* Of course.

Man Who Speaks Somewhere In Between The
Second And Third Person Omniscient: *(aka* Ezra*)*
Thanks. I appreciate it.

Beth: The way it was told to me someone heard
strange scratching noises
coming from my daughter Shawn's room,
so they went to investigate.

Aaron: …a roasted suckling pig with an apple
impaled in // its mouth.

Beth: They couldn't quite make out the noise
even though she was just on the other side of the door.

Aaron: …It's not just that his face is grave, it's that it's
become a grave//stone

Beth: Thinking he had an emergency on his hands,
He shouldered the door open.
And inside the room… my god

SHAWN: I've found it:
The keystone

BETH: Paper everywhere.
Notes, research materials,
Legal pads filled with illegible handwriting.

SHAWN: The magic shard of kryptonite

BETH: Dirty clothes….

HENRY: CHARLIE ROSE begins the introduction of his
guest // holding a copy of her book

BETH: Window wide open with white curtains
billowing in the breeze

HENRY: A few drops of Merlot savagely contrast // the
white of the carpet.

BETH: A total mess.
But no Shawn.
She'd vanished into thin air.

SHAWN: AARON:
The cat burglar's pick   OSCAR's middle and
                              forefinger go limp

BETH: She hadn't even come close to finishing chapter
seven. She'd barely started it.
There were hundreds of pages of barely legible
senseless scrawl written on Legal pads…

SHAWN: AARON:
That once turned   The cigar slips

BETH: The only thing anyone could make out in all
those pages was a single word

SHAWN: will drop the tumblers // in place…

AARON: Like the rotor of a doomed helicopter.

BETH: A single word written clearly on the very last
page Shawn wrote.

SHAWN: Opening a door…

BETH: She wrote:

BETH & SHAWN: "Cohiba"

HENRY: Everything goes black. The En—

10

WOMAN WHO SPEAKS IN THE SECOND PERSON
OMNISCIENT: *(aka* KATE*)* Now seems like an appropriate
time to segue into scene ten.

MAN WHO SPEAKS SOMEWHERE IN BETWEEN THE
SECOND AND THIRD PERSON OMNISCIENT: *(aka* EZRA*)*
The final scene in which Jessica attempts to reconstruct
the contents of her murdered sister's diary.

*(*JESSICA *appears, dressed differently than before—a make
over that makes her resemble Shawn, as she was "dressed"
by* AARON *and* HENRY *for the Charlie Rose sequence.)*

JESSICA: As far as I can tell,
my sister never wrote another word in her diary.
I don't know for certain if
she ever worked up the nerve to
see G. in New Haven.
And "G"
Well
He refuses to return my calls.
My emails.
Letters I've written him.
I suppose some people prefer silence over truth.

What I can say for certain is
The morning of her murder I
Wasn't feeling well. I hadn't been feeling well for
several mornings.
Fearing the worst I
I took a pregnancy test....
My boyfriend Rob and I...

we weren't ready for kids.
We were perfectly content living together
without having marriage get in the way.
I was struggling through grad school.
Rob was working temp jobs…

That night we were up late packing for a trip to
Chicago,
For yes,
Dad's annual Cigar Party.
Almost exactly a year to the day after the one my sister
wrote about in her diary….

Things were tense between Rob and me—
Me for obvious reasons,
Rob, because he felt that Dad, Mom, my sister and her
hus—
The man who murdered her—
Went out of their way to make us feel uncomfortable
About the life we'd chosen.
Those choices didn't compute in their world
That frustrated Rob.
Me too.

I have to say—
And this is
the most difficult thing
to admit
But
That night,
I actually said to Rob that
I couldn't bear the thought
of spending a night in my sister's presence
feeling as inadequate as she made me feel
She was the brilliant one. The beautiful one. The
successful one.
The one with the *perfect* marriage…

Then the words just fell out of my mouth.
"Rob. I'm pregnant."

That moment,
two thousand miles away
That monster
who'd vowed to love and to honor her
To cherish her in sickness and in health
Murdered my sister.
Murdered her
And the baby she was carrying inside of her.

I spend lots of nights sleepless
Wondering
What kind of relationship my sister and I might've had
Had we known that we were both carrying children at
the same time.

Maybe she would have shared her most private fears
with me
Instead of keeping them buried in the pages of her
diary.
Maybe I could have forged a real relationship to her in
life
Rather than forging the one I now have with her in
death.

(An INTERVIEWER *appears.)*

INTERVIEWER: And you had twins.

JESSICA: Yes. Joshua and Alex.

INTERVIEWER: I understand you've seen the film.

JESSICA: Yes.

INTERVIEWER: Not an easy experience…?

JESSICA: No. That would be an understatement.

INTERVIEWER: I'm going to
Read to you a
passage from the original screenplay

one of the
flashbacks
that repeats throughout the film.
"We see the WOMAN, visibly pregnant. Tears of
frustration and humiliation rain down her face."
"She watches her HUSBAND, at the fireplace, tearing
pages from the diary one by one, and throwing them
into the flames."
Reaction.

JESSICA: My reaction?
I felt a lot of things.
Pain. Anger. I felt violated. I felt like
"why am I watching this why am I putting myself
through this"
But at the same time there was this
Remove.

INTERVIEWER: "Remove". Talk about that.

JESSICA: I already had an excruciatingly vivid movie
branded into my brain about what happened.
In that movie it's my real sister I see. Not some famous
actress.
In that movie it's
him
I see. In all his monstrosity.
Not some handsome matinee idol testing his range as
an actor.
Compared to the movie in my mind,
The film's pretty—
I'm afraid the young men who made the film have no
experience with true horror.

INTERVIEWER: I'd like to address one of the more…
Controversial
Aspects of the film for you.
Shawn.

JESSICA: What about her.

INTERVIEWER: Given she's central to the film…

JESSICA: Like the rest of the film, she's a fiction.

INTERVIEWER: She was a student of your father's.
More than a student that she was

JESSICA: His protégé?
Mister Miller and Mister Blumenthal are in the fiction-
making business.

INTERVIEWER: Since the film's release you've
Become quite active.
You've published your sister's diary.
You've given interviews.
You have your own website.

JESSICA: That's correct.

INTERVIEWER: I read somewhere you're giving a lecture
tour of colleges this fall.

JESSICA: Is there a question this is leading to?
My sister was murdered.
My twins won't ever know their aunt.
I will never hear my sister's voice again.
She can't speak for herself anymore.
And the film
The film doesn't speak for her.
Someone has to speak for her.

INTERVIEWER: I read that you've expressed
disappointment with some of the film's casting
choices—in particular the actress chosen to play you.

JESSICA: That's ridiculous. I'm not even going to dignify
that.

WOMAN WHO SPEAKS IN THE SECOND PERSON
OMNISCIENT: (aka KATE) Somewhere her sister weeps
Tears of frustration and humiliation rain down her
face.

MAN WHO SPEAKS SOMEWHERE IN BETWEEN THE
SECOND AND THIRD PERSON OMNISCIENT: *(aka* EZRA*)*
She watches her husband
Standing next to the fireplace in the living room of
their home
Staring at her silently
WOMAN WHO SPEAKS IN THE SECOND PERSON
OMNISCIENT: *(aka* KATE*)* Tearing pages from a book
One
By
One.
And throwing them into the flames.

MAN WHO SPEAKS SOMEWHERE IN BETWEEN THE
SECOND AND THIRD PERSON OMNISCIENT: *(aka* EZRA*)*
Each time he tears into the book
She feels his fingers tear into her
Ripping out chunks of her flesh.
He tosses the binding of the diary into the fire

WOMAN WHO SPEAKS IN THE SECOND PERSON
OMNISCIENT: *(aka* KATE*)* The binding takes longer than
the pages to turn into ash.

MAN WHO SPEAKS SOMEWHERE IN BETWEEN THE
SECOND AND THIRD PERSON OMNISCIENT: *(aka* EZRA*)*
Now he just stares at her

WOMAN WHO SPEAKS IN THE SECOND PERSON
OMNISCIENT: *(aka* KATE*)* Breathing like a wild animal

MAN WHO SPEAKS SOMEWHERE IN BETWEEN THE
SECOND AND THIRD PERSON OMNISCIENT: *(aka* EZRA*)*
Knuckles white as they grip
The iron poker from the fireplace.
(He raises the iron poker above his head, about to strike,
when…)

(Blackout)

11

WOMAN WHO SPEAKS IN THE SECOND
PERSON OMNISCIENT: *(aka* KATE*)*
Thetruthbehindbeforeandafterdotcom: an epilogue
It's two forty-seven am and you're home.
You spent the evening with a close friend
having dinner and seeing *before and after*
The new film by Aaron Miller and Henry Blumenthal.
Afterwards,
You engaged in a lively discussion of the film
at a bar near the movie theatre.
You loved the film,
your friend, she hated it,
the bartender chimed in—
He was neither here nor there about it.

After drinks with your friend
You arrive home half past midnight.
You check your voice mail,
You take the dog out for a squirt.
Not quite ready to sleep
You pour yourself a glass of wine,
And turn on C N N.
At one thirty,
You turn off your television
and head to your bedroom.
You lay down , turn out the lights,
And close your eyes hoping sleep will find you.

After tossing and turning
You emerge from your bedroom.
You pour yourself another glass of wine.
And sit in the darkness.

You worry about money.
You worry about the relationship you're in
You worry about whether the life you are leading is the
life you wanted.

You pour yourself another glass of wine.
Your thoughts shift to *before and after*.
You remember being struck by the power of the film.
The well-observed performances, the crafty
camerawork.
The tense and dissonant beauty of the film's score
You remember noting in the opening credits
That the screenplay is based on a true story.

In an effort to cure your insomnia
You pour yourself another glass of wine
And turn on your computer.
You Google the name of the film.
You find a virtual encyclopedia of information on the
film
But nothing on the film's true-life sources.
Until,
You stumble upon a link:
Double u double u double u
Thetruthbehindbeforeandafter
dot
com.
You click on the link.

A splash page appears on your screen.
The word "before" fades in,
Grey, like a distant childhood memory,
"before".
Followed by the word "after"—
Bold, in all caps,
Indelible, like the etching of a date on a gravestone.
"AFTER"

Photographs fill the white spaces.
On the "before" half of the screen:
unremarkable snapshots of the real-life Oscar, Marisol,
Jessica,
and her murdered sister

On the "after" half of the screen:
Stills from the motion picture.
Dramatic.
Slickly lit.
Flawlessly composed.

The final photos depict the crime scene.
On the "before" half of the screen, a photo from the
coroner's camera,
Clinical,
artless,
a half naked woman's body covered in a blanket
stained in blood.
An iron poker on the carpet.
On the "after" half of the screen,
Photos of an actress,
Posing as a corpse,
A goddess that died beautiful.

Below the photo gallery,
another set of words:
before and after: the true story behind the film.
click to enter.

You know now that sleep tonight is out of the question.
You pour yourself another glass of wine.
You follow the instruction on screen—
Clicking your mouse to enter this rabbit hole.

END OF PLAY

www.ingramcontent.com/pod-product-compliance
Lightning Source LLC
Chambersburg PA
CBHW052203090426
42741CB00010B/2393